Orang

poems by

Christy Bailes

Finishing Line Press
Georgetown, Kentucky

Orang

For Mom and Dad
For Sandy
For Melissa
For Ann
For my sacred circle of cycling buddies

Copyright © 2021 by Christy Bailes
ISBN 978-1-64662-586-4 First Edition
All rights reserved under International and Pan-American Copyright Conventions. No part of this book may be reproduced in any manner whatsoever without written permission from the publisher, except in the case of brief quotations embodied in critical articles and reviews.

ACKNOWLEDGMENTS

The author wishes to thank the editors of the following journals in which these poems first appeared, sometimes in different form:

Abstract Magazine: "Because I Could Not Stop the Pics," "Purex Imagination"
Calaveras Station Arts & Literary Journal: "Sonnet on a Sloth," "Teaching Water Aerobics"
Dovecote Magazine: "Biking Drunk"
Gyroscope Review: "A Message from Mary"
Havik: "Dying in Your Sixties"
Inkwell Journal: "Idée Fixe"
Pamplemousse: "Exam"
Panoply: "Dying in Paradise"
The Penmen Review: "Bluestocking," "A Sonnet to Shakespeare"
San Joaquin Review: "Chicken of the Trees"
Suisun Valley Review: "'Unfortunately, Your Poem Is Not the Right Fit'"
The Finger Literary Journal: "Liminal Lane"
Wingless Dreamer: "The Crying Clarinet"

I wish to thank Lynne Knight, Patrick Culliton, Sandra Dutton, Darcy Schultz, Mike Williams, and Joshua McKinney for their immense support and encouragement throughout the shaping of this book.

Publisher: Leah Huete de Maines
Editor: Christen Kincaid
Cover Art: Christy Bailes
Author Photo: Christy Bailes
Cover Design: Elizabeth Maines McCleavy

Order online: www.finishinglinepress.com
also available on amazon.com

Author inquiries and mail orders:
Finishing Line Press
PO Box 1626
Georgetown, Kentucky 40324
USA

Table of Contents

On a Good Day 1

Idée Fixe 3

Chicken of the Trees 5

Teaching Water Aerobics 7

"Unfortunately, Your Poem Is Not the Right Fit" 9

Bluestocking 11

The Crying Clarinet 12

How to Smoke 14

Art Against Art 15

To Deny Which Is 17

A Poet's Life 18

Biking Drunk 20

A Message from Mary 22

Exam 24

If You Think You Should 26

Sonnet on a Sloth 27

A Sonnet to Shakespeare 28

Addictive Benediction 29

Purex Imagination 31

Liminal Lane 32

On a Good Day

I crack open a Diet Coke
      and raise my can
    to the smoking hot blonde
lighting up the sky.

If only I had better integument
      for the superstar
    whose happy gas
makes me think we're twins,

except for those days
     when she plays old films
with messy lines or dots
       on low-hanging clouds.

But I don't like to speak of her
    when she's not out front
singing salsa music
      with a wide vibrato.

In fact, I don't want
    to go outside
  if I don't need protection
for my bold nose.

I must have
the kind of day
     where she licks my skin
with her chili tongue

penetrating my piggy pigment
     through sun sleeves
and 100 SPF,
     where she's determined

to turn me into
    a red pepper
out of sheer love
      for the freckled mess

splattered all over my limbs.
    I know she knows
how much I need her
   solar sauce.

Idée Fixe

My senescent dad picks up sticks
in a plaid dressing gown
and talks like a baby to Tuxy,
who trails behind his shuffling steps.
Cat talk, he calls it.

When he runs out of sticks,
                he climbs the extension ladder
                  with fearless feebleness by
                      stepping around rungs and onto the roof
                        to push pine needles off the ledge.
He waves and grins,
terrifying neighbors,
who yell, *Get down from there!*

Mom's a nervous wreck,
                poking her head out
                each hour
                like a cuckoo,
                checking on her doddering groom,
but then she goes back to
                        decorating some holiday with more holiday.

Like always, he escapes the roof
and enters the junk jungle,
                pushing his paunch
                through whatever time of year
happens to be inside the house,
                passing remote shelves
of pressed glass, cut glass, carnival glass, milk glass, cranberry
glass, and depression glass;
but he doesn't see *his* stranded antiques,
                he sees
mom's jewelry hanging
                like crows' meat
          in the crowded hallway
              as he moves through
      humming fluorescents.

Having heard dad's dynamic door slam, mom knows he's off the roof.
    She opens the door to my old bedroom
        and squeezes through boxes stacked to the ceiling
      to look for   a decorative decoy
      decaying in the dangerous
        entrapment of her lost childhood.
   .

While mom digs, dad finally makes it to the bathroom.
    He powders himself
        and everything else
with talcum powder from London,
    then scoots and arranges and replaces
        thrift store stuff
    with other
thrift store stuff,
    which is stuffed in every drawer.

Near the end of his daily ritual,
he admires his hypotactic décor
    from a commode's view
        with a Marilyn Monroe clock on the right,
an Aristotle sculpture on the left,
    and a small wooden Jesus behind
        to absolve
          their festive mess.

Chicken of the Trees

> *Iguanas are falling from trees due to cold weather. National Weather Service assured that they are not dead, just cold*
> —Ella Torres, ABC News

According to the internet,
I suffer from doormat mindset,
as if adding a psychosomatic word
will make it sound less terrible.

The truth is, we all lie
under someone's foot
one time or another,
but I always seem to be

the mat under the mat under the mat,
the most worn, the most trampled
without being seen, except
on a rare, deep-cleaning day.

Do you know what it's like?
Do you? To be picked
as third choice
on a cold day when Iguanas

fall from trees, not dead
but motionless with hands
in the air and up for grabs
for good Florida grilling.

I would be so lucky
to have a skewer through my
stocky spines and heavy jowls
instead of strolling soles on my face.

Let's face it, when do you wipe your feet?
When you've stepped in dog doo?
When you've stepped in a puddle?

Well, I tell you this:
I am going to be a giant green lizard,
eating your ornamental plants

and sunning myself silly,
but if the temperature drops again,
you may eat my delicacy.

Teaching Water Aerobics

I'm sopped
    in a soupy bowl
        of chloramines
with Great Grannies sitting on noodles
            as their flaggy flaps
    attempt jumping jacks

when
a shaky lady sends her snake
        skyrocketing,
    and she falls backwards.
Her mouth opens and closes like a fish
facing the sky
        needing oxygen.

My fingers lock, forcing me
    to hide the senior's throat
in the crook of my elbow,
        dragging her,

but she's so slippery
    she falls through,
        sinking. I go under
to get her, but I forget to open my eyes.

I swat with stony bones
    in the elders' water
trying to find her without sight,
    afraid to catch her, afraid she'll die.

        Then I remember to open my eyes;
the sodden cod thrashes,
        flounders, fights
unable to remember
her way out of
        her sunken submarine.

I finally catch the old lady
                    and bring her to the surface
            where I see
                    my suicidal fish I couldn't save
reflecting in her
            upside-down eyes.

"Unfortunately, Your Poem Is Not the Right Fit"

If only you were one of my star-struck grannies
sitting with medicinal gin after attending my aqua aerobics class,
                      you'd think I was great
no matter what
           giving me slobbery comments
                  on
              each post.

You'd read every syllable
           and dance in your chair
with diuretics on your breath,
        convinced I'd invented verse.

"Read this," you'd scream
in your husband's ear
        spitting nothing but air,
although he wouldn't hear a word you said.

For an hour, you'd share
   my poem
a thousand times,
       commenting on comments of comments
until you've exhausted yourself.

After a nap or two,
you'd start again,
           except this time
on your flip phone
      messaging friends
that I posted the greatest poem,
           even though you can't remember when.

That's how it is with my elderly fans.

So, I say this to you, my editor,
pretend you're old with a couple of chins
                                      and publish my poem.

But I guess you'll pass this time around,
        as you usually do
    with the words,
"I want to make it clear
I enjoyed your work."

Bluestocking

She was put together so lovely
in a black-and-white dress,
then she turned away,
revealing tousled hair,
as if to invite boundless art.

Trying to make my smile fall,
I covered my face,
and listened to whispers
containing blue, the color
of her eyes under

literary charm, as she
sprinkled blue chips,
blue blood, like word dust
from fingers long enough
to write meaning on my heart.

Who says English can't sail
blue waters? Her class
taught life in synonyms,
strong enough to sway
me down the writing path.

The Crying Clarinet

I can't get to my licorice stick,
      even though I taste
   bitter reed in my sleep.

"Don't let the light dim,"
        my friend said yesterday,
           as I finger the air

like I'm already dead,
     even though a few ears
rest against my bell.

I promise to pick it up again
      after I graduate
      with another creative writing degree,

but I don't think I can wait
    with such a weepy tone
keeping me up at night.

I wasn't great but good,
   so I had to seek
smiles elsewhere,

as if poetry
      would be a better way
to receive praise.

Computer keys
    hardly compare
to dark wood
and its forsaken melodies

haunting me
with every word I type
    because my larynx
sits in a dusty case.

So I suffer
as the moan of rich molasses
    begs my presence
before my hands
        disappear.

How to Smoke

My swift talking licker
laps against night
    in a fire I fired
      with broken lyres from
              wanting word-wizard fame.
It's simple. It really is. I
play with smoke
              shapeshifting
    my craft
    into cloud-like nouveau.
How the haze swirls
    a temporal phrase
through the flame
    of my ghost,
as if I'm dead, rotted, and gone,
dropping
        syntactic ashes
      over some stuffed
             scholastic arm.
I pack my pyre
    with scatting sticks,
staging the all-mighty: signifier and signifried
    to ignite
      a shifty trick.
Then when my hoax
    begins to smoke,
      I sculpt
a crepitating tale
    with my tattle-tongue
still telling about how
    only words escaped.

Art Against Art

A professor once told me
        to "write faster."
                If it were that easy,
I would spend less time
        in a poetic coma.

Sure, it looks like
I do a lot of nothing in my gaze,
        but really,
              words reside in stillness.

My creativity will haul off and hit
    my gut
        if I crack an egg
                over a cloud.

Like today, it's 75 and partly blah
compared to
how perfect I felt yesterday
        sitting on the swing with my dog
            after I did a photo shoot for my social media post.

And now, I can hardly bear
    the wind
making the branches giggle
outside my bedroom window.

This nice day hurts,
        tripping over
             every hour.

I cannot exercise
I cannot repeat the Nebraska summer hot look
        while jealous words hate
        how successful I was twenty-four hours ago
in a patriotic knit top and platform sandals
with a flowing brown wig.

So, I stare, and type
a few terrible ideas
until a comment pops up
        like a marquee.
It reads, "Seriously, Lady, how many looks do you have?"
Maybe, the professor was right.
    I should "write faster,"
        although I might add,
    "even if you have to change face."

To Deny Which Is

Upon further consideration,
    I am not like an orangutan,
  except for being born with orange hair.

I don't swing from trees.
I don't live a solitary existence.

But I'll be damned if Poe's "Morgue Murders"
    didn't give me the wrong impression
of an ape.

I thought it a hairy beast
beating its four hands
      against my ribs
   every time I had an urge
        to be bad,

and by bad, I mean drinking dirty martinis
    at a local hang
      only to wake up to
my bike in pieces
on the kitchen floor.

Maybe, I got it all wrong.
Maybe, I have overgrown branches in my chest.

As it turns out, I need
my strong strapping
    Orang
to show me how
to live in trees
   with only rain in my cup.

Don't misunderstand.
It's more the urge
  to be bad than drink,
    and I will go so far as to say
the word "bad" really means
              free.

A Poet's Life

Out last night with friends
    in a cozy saloon in Suisun Valley,
        I lapsed into
            narrating my eulogy,
just in case I expired before I should.
It started something like,
    "She once said every day should be a holiday. So let's not be sad; let's
        get up and dance and celebrate. She would have wanted it that way. And please, choose
      your favorite festive beads—she had them all. And wear them as she would have worn
        them if she could have been here."

With liquored-up laughs, they received my memorial better than I expected
            until the practical one said, "Aren't you going to be buried in Florida?"
            The other friend said, "You could be sprinkled, a little here,
        a little there. Then you could make yourself available for everyone."

Such ridiculous funerary talk warranted another round,
    so we motioned for the owner,
   who tended to us at once.
  He's the reason the three of us come back week after week,
drink after drink.

We looked up to him,
as if he were Hercules,
            commanding every ear
   with great stories. People flocked to his words
and majestic face,
                for he has managed quite a feat
teaching college psych and running a bar.

He knows how to treat humans,
delivering himself with our drinks in his round, black spectacles,
            and so, he began to tell us about his morning:

"Our two-year-old daughter woke us this morning to tell us she was ugly. I hopped out of bed to get to the bottom of it. After doing an inquiry, my son admitted that he had called himself ugly the other day."

I raised my hand, interrupting his story to say,
            "Your little girl just demonstrated Lacan's 'Mirror Stage' theory."
He tilted his demigod head
until a smile broke through,
                and I fell from the bar stool, spilling Mardi Gras beads
all over the floor.

Biking Drunk

Barely able to stand,
                I put the bike
between my legs
and pray
    to be an eagle's feather
        for all eternity.

There's a charge in the air,
   as endorphins
mute my cowbell heart
   and offer the words

light as a feather, stiff as a drink.

To the people in cars,
I look like every other cyclist
   switching gears
 with precision and ease
     in a colorful jersey and padded bike shorts.

                   They either love us
                      or hate us
by riding so close
    we choke
        on carbon monoxide.

                   But it doesn't matter—
                   I can't feel my arms or legs.

What creaks underneath
enables the momentum,
    the enabler I pair with wine

better than cheese or sex
      because I float freestyle
            with a Merlot mustache
after being
part of a heavy head and hooked beak
     during the work week
            when I don't
     have legs
         running down
        the side
         of my glass.

A Message from Mary

It's a Saturday for the holiest of creatures,
and here I sit
        because my biking buddy has a catarrh.

Sure, I was invited to go on a group hike
    to learn about birds as bards,
        but all be damned if I can't trust my tibia
    to withstand terrain's torment
          for seven miles,

and if that's not enough,
        I sprained my wrist
      from sleeping.

It has come to writing my life better than it is,
    although Mary Oliver's bird just flew into my bedroom window,
unnerving my cat
        and splatting my pane
            just to tell me, "Don't do that."

So I will tell you what you don't want to hear:
The spirit gets stronger as your soma slips into disrepair,
        laming one limb at a time
      although I shouldn't complain,
            I have run four marathons and ridden across Iowa.

But I want more.
            I want to run half-marathons again.
           I want to bike across the United States
        and sleep in a hammock suspended between trees,
           rather than
debating such a sad writing idea as
        whether a washer can erase memories from clothes.

I'd rather
        be
                raising brawny biceps with a rough cry
over a finish line
                      or rolling through small towns
            with a proud, distinctive stench.

"Give me birds or give me death,"
                I say,
as I hope to ride my life better than this.

Exam

1. If a man sits in the last row of an aircraft and a lady reclines her seat, he should:
a. Punch her seat repeatedly
b. Punch her repeatedly
c. Drink Paper Plane Punch without Amero and Aperol
d. Put on some headphones, listen to his favorite tunes, and find his ride

2. If Mom finds a fat-shaming note in her kid's lunch box, she should:
a. Give the teacher a wedgie
b. Help her kid find his ride
c. Slander the school's name
d. Post the story on social media for all eternity

3. If a teenager violates the "no turn on red sign" at an intersection, the male bicyclist should:
a. Throw a bike lock at the car
b. Chase the car down
c. Kick the phone from the passenger's hand before she takes a picture of him
d. Choose a different ride

4. If a woman spills hot coffee on her lap at a drive-thru window, she should:
a. Sue the fast-food chain
b. Throw her empty cup at the attendant
c. Laugh and continue her ride
d. Curse her worst words

5. If you're highly intoxicated, you should not
a.   Call 911 to tell the dispatcher that your wife is a "black widow spider"
b.
c.   Ride a lawnmower, combine, or motorized scooter on an interstate
d.   Call 911 if you are underage and can't get an attendant to sell you more beer

6. If you suffer, you should:
a.   Find your ride
b.   Find your ride
c.   Find your ride
d.   Find your ride

7. If a police therapy dog steals toys for a charity, you should:
a.   Take away the toys
b.   Make a bed of toys
c.   Learn from the dog
d.   Both b and c

If You Think You Should

go ahead
                  and wed
a bride or groom
                but have a broom, please
                              have   a   broom,

no, not a broom, but a field of hay
      and stuff   your shirt
                    your pants
                    your brain
                    and prepare to stay,
    scaring every bird
                      with your married face.

You might get lucky,
                  although it could get ugly,
                        losing to
the louse's law
          of
              Take it all.

But go ahead and bed
              your newlywed
until the banging stops
                  and you become
    a dusty dummy
                  ditched in a field of dismay.

It'll be the worst,
            the worst it'll be
if your
                hay
            goes
                      up
          in
              flames.

Sonnet on a Sloth

Shall I compare thee to a three-toed sloth?
Your wookiee smile hip hops in camouflage,
among the coco palms, and drips hot broth,
more delicious than a furry tree corsage.
Such tender prongs you wear on pitchfork feet,
to keep the fronds unharmed from storms ground-up.
You drop four-on-the-shore to swim a beat
and school the wookiee with the hottest strut.
On land away from me, you shake so lean
at ninety degrees from ground, where algae hums
an elegy, crawling to swoon the sylvan queen,
and you, so tall, expect my battered drums.
The wookiee be my lawful sloth henceforth;
I will not beat, not now, not ever more!

A Sonnet to Shakespeare

If I be your mistress, hand me the sun;
let my red lips leave a kiss on your skin.
If I be snow, touch my sweet cherry breasts,
crisp delicacies for you to taste.
If wires be rough on your scratchy face;
let them catch on my shiny, golden hair,
falling over delicious apple cheeks.
If your breath be reeking, take mine in yours
until ocean mist sprays our coral mouths.
If I play clarinet, move my thin hips
to pastoral songs as sweet as my voice
that whisper my body into your ear.
And yet, you are not blinded by true love,
if you were, you'd think hot my beauty be.

Addictive Benediction

My lips warm the softest metal
with a thousand sexy sips a day.

           You will tell me I drink poison
                and how sad it is
                      that I can't stop.

But you must know,
I panic when I think of going to Europe or surgery
          without my twenty-four companions.

I cannot live one minute without
                sweet little balls of bubbles
      bouncing down my windpipe.

Oh how I hold the can,
snuggling its cozy coat in both hands
         as if it were coffee,
         except for the residual red stripe
                    seducing me to its spout.

I ascribe holy blessedness,
    to the last drop of aspartame,
        only to have Sulfuric Sissy nearby
along with her cousins Carmela Color and bossy Potassium Benzoate.

In fact, I will have drunk the whole family
by the end of the day,
wearing more smiles than
        those who drink Spring from a bottle.

I sup a new season,
where battery acid caffeinates
                every pastoral organ.

                            But go ahead and tell me
                                        to quit,
        for to quit
        would keep
                so many silvery-white sweethearts
                            from falling upon my face.

Purex Imagination

In these viral times, be as bold as you can be
and even bolder still until sun shines where darkness hides.
Walk with me without me near, and I will do the same.
We've got this, friends, even behind so much shade.
The holy bus of your belief will stop, if you flag it down.
Get inside and hold on tight and tighter still until you feel calm.
Keep this calm, nurture it however you can,
so the bus will drop you off near nature's noisiest frog.
Then, crowd a flower, get in its way, and breathe. Don't forget to
breathe.
But don't linger too long. You must find trees
to walk you down a path and fill your breath,
fuller than before. Take it in, take it all in
as nature washes what sanitizer can't. When you're ready,
open your eyes, call everyone you love.

Liminal Lane

It occurred to me this morning
that I have eggshells for joints,
but I dare say, I don't need new
hardware yet,

like the hip my friend just got,
along with a certificate
for participating in the
joint replacement program.

I just know I will need
to replace my
pretty patella.
But I will not want

an award—I have plenty.
I will ask doctors for pics
to show how runners' rage
ruins cartilage from pounding

the ground with problems.
Still, I continue, wondering
if I'm moving anything
but walled-in will.

If I could, I would ask
for my knee, so I could
display it like grotesque art.
It turns out though,

the bone remains in place,
while the doc puts a jaunty cap
made of metal or plastic
on the resurfaced knee joint.

Doesn't sound terrible,
in fact, maybe I would
be bionic and badass again.
Until then, maybe you

will see me shuffling
with a distinctive head bobble
unable to rend the division
between walking and running.

Originally from St. Petersburg, Florida, Christy Bailes lives in Fairfield, California. After retiring from the Air Force Band of the Golden West, she attended California State University, Sacramento and received her second master's degree in creative writing. Her work has appeared or is forthcoming in *Suisun Valley Review, Havik, The Finger, Abstract Magazine, San Joaquin Review, Gyroscope Review, Dovecote Magazine, Panoply, Pamplemousse, Calaveras Station Literary Journal, The Penmen Review, Inkwell Journal,* and *Wingless Dreamer*. She has also won an honorable mention twice in the Mattia International Poetry Contest. In 2016, she received a master's degree in creative writing from Southern New Hampshire University. Her poetry teachers include Lynne Knight, Patrick Culliton, and Joshua McKinney. In 1993, she obtained a bachelor's degree from Eastman School of Music in clarinet performance. Besides writing poetry and playing music, she teaches Water Aerobics at three different aquatic centers and inspires others to lead a healthy lifestyle. In her free time, she uses running and cycling to fuel her creativity.

www.ingramcontent.com/pod-product-compliance
Lightning Source LLC
LaVergne TN
LVHW041602070426
835507LV00011B/1269